VINCENT BOZZINO

THE JOY OF MISSING OUT

LIBERTINE PRESS

© 2023 Vincent Bozzino

Libertine Press
34 Berkley Square
London, UK W1J 5BF

www.libertinepress.com

All rights reserved. No part of this book may be reproduced or used in any manner, without written permission except in the case of brief quotations embodied in social media, critical articles and book reviews.

First published, 2023

Originally written in 2013, with the working title "The Rose and the Mole".
Last of the *"Youth Poems"* trilogy.

Printed by IngramSpark/Lighting Source in UK
San Francisco Layout
Concept, Cover Art by Vincent Bozzino

Paperback ISBN 978-1-7392377-7-6
Ebook ISBN 978-1-7392377-8-3

A catalogue record for this title is available from the British Library.

THE JOY OF MISSING OUT

To my failures
Cheers

α

Sweet is my surrender
Most mornings
To being less than others
To my joy of being sad
- how many things I lost
and how many I don't have -
To my strength in finding beauty
Even where there is none

β

The window

Easy semblance it seemed
to change space into nothing
when nothing coloured space before me

After the slamming of the doors
here is the shaken son
in the crowd a father escaped me suddenly

Satisfied only by my bed
my bright eyes dead
amidst family's quarrels and problems

But my pencil is silly, passionate and deep
The only who has promises to keep

ע

Behind the pressure of the wage
The washing blood of sleep
A dry mouth eats
That only at sea can rest a little
Alas
Resilience is the key to the world

6

When I began to think of troubles
On that day my soul grew hard
'Life!' chuckled I, *'Yes death!'*
I awoke and flung the clothes
I sat unengaged and afflicted
My passion is the smelly woe
Once upon a midnight missing
Deep into my brain malfunctioning
Disorder
Much, endless
Concerning, hurting, risking
Ever so fabricated

―――――――――――――――

3

Special captive of dirt
you are a very modest mole
and you do not live off worms alone
you jump the crumbling quagmire
of simple animal life
and you make paths, toward the horizon
where there aren't, in the unknown dawn
Take root in darkness
and treasure the maze of your lairs
for the superb rose you wish to conquer
and without digging in doubt
you already see the long-awaited petal.

_____

༗

You turn upside down in her thorns
while not claiming pain
waiting for the love to change life
with bright, red petals
and spin by day
and spin by night
to see his buttocks again
reflection in a mirror
and pretend this is not a spiderweb

η

Now that I live September
in the loony sleeping of leaves
do not follow my ruby cloak
just to be able to get rich.
Swarming with broken-wing fairies is
the gray soul of yours
drenched in greed
aged by the thief of parade.
Now you brag of the plastic
and hide in the show of nullity
Lady, come as you are

θ

Spring Time
And I'm not blooming again
But I don't mind
My flair for impotence
The joy of missing out
And spending time with compassion for my climb
When most only get the dark
Why do I fight my light within

―――――――――――

ι

And there's you and me in my dreams,
only us,
sat on the roof of the world
waiting for a shooting star
there's only you and me in the motels,
in the alleys, on the sheets
to enjoy each other
only us,
stretched out at the gates of a dream
perhaps, made of cardboard
because it has crumbled
love is a sweet pile of stones
where the heart seats.

к

Respecting the Winter inside

Black sheets, without curtains,
the silence of wheat
warms up my August
I already feel
the burned shores of my fortune

White sheets, pale noon resting
the beaches and mopeds in circle
I sense September hurdles
for my being content never starts

Blue sheets, caresses of the years,
the distant claws of the sea
glue my eyes to another sunrise
that fires and fades my cravings

λ

Agility stalks true genius
Who thrives on intelligence
Because he doesn't know what to do with just one
The miserable unnerving search for a stage
A larger gallows though
Where to reign and offer art to the peoples
For life
This suffocates him in a horrendous grip
completely incomplete
In the queue, though
Here is the bewildering constant of his mornings
Getting out of its natural shell of ubiquity
To choose the light of success or the shadow of anonymity
And then trouble
With the hope of taking flight one day
Or the fear of staying on the ground forever
The terror of becoming someone
Or staying someone else

μ

I have no best
Nothing but music
The world is full of beautiful girls
And my head is full of insecurity
That's why I can't win you over
And I like staying here

―――――――

ʋ

Lying on the last branch of the oldest tree
Barefoot thrown into the void
I lost my shoes
They fell too soon
Before the others
The leaves tremble when my hand does
Burned alive on an invisible stake
I am
What job will I have?
The twin sun of six comes to keep me company
I haven't seen the horizon for months
I don't know whose will be my next breath
You know, it hasn't belonged to me for a long time
The soul of a rebel poet
The air of a time that gives me nothing
Sun in the north, cruelty in luggage to be lost immediately
Before the shoes come back
Revenge, violence, forgiveness and peace, anger.
I guess it reflects my mood
A white elephant
Is this alienation or is it not?

ξ

And in the days of old
when granny dug up the buckets,
Small farms were slaughtering
bovines and other crops
the survival economy was feeling good
But we now despise to dig the buckets
rather feed with synthetic proteins
Body as a machine
Coffins closer than it seems

[Hunger]

―――――――――――

o

As snow does to a fire, through splendid cities
Mankind sucks joyfully
All the oleanders, every each skull
Like dragonflies brushing on drowning
For more than a thousand years

On the clear summer evenings
One-armed friends
World is on a journey
Down a dead end
On golden chariot
Manipulated paladins are marching
School is hell-bent
A horror of sick mind games

Earth is a small rustle of wings
Noisy black puppets
Weep on government's shoulders
Blood of green trees but endless

The rivers let me sail
I have felt warmth eternal

VINCENT BOZZINO

Warning men and women
Still, a flock of doves
Folks sank
Down into abysses
A thousand mistakes yet we never learn

[How the earth is a small rustle of wings]

π

How sweet is surrender
Laid from work or school, I saw no fate
When we force some cruel defence to life
As fast as a smile it fades

Freedom and beauty have once their gold
We must bend ourselves to be its hog
Hoping the vast back of our wings unfold
When morning tea speaks in a bitter cup

ρ

Often the most desired pale things
die on one's garment
desperate from the formless labor
often they fade out in the stars
or only take shelter
In hope for a sudden expectation
Why don't we like to wait anymore?

Σ

In fields of jungle, where flamingos dance and sway
A gentle threat caresses every stem
The money too threats us with weeks of gray
And birdsong fills the air but we no longer hear them

Oh, how the beauty of the world may fade
And nothing's left between sorrow and regret
But lo, a slice of health may fairly persuade
A heart to beat and not to fret

For crisis is like a seed that grows so strong
Its roots run deep, its branches reach up high
But though a year's journey may be hard and long
A purpose will move us to fight for our why

Let us cherish every moment dear
And hold our loved ones close, forever near

τ

In the midst of the stillness
A void so profound
Endless darkness surrounds
Numbness without a ground

The emptiness within me
A chasm so wide
An abyss I cannot cross
But my ego shows off outside

The club feels so hollow,
A colorless scene
Too much emotion I felt
A lifelessness routine

The silence echoes loudly
A persistent break
Loneliness consumes me
And I never pray

Yet my plans are eternal
I see light in the dark

VINCENT BOZZINO

A promise of renewal
A journey I embark

So I'll keep on moving
Through this emptiness vast
For beyond this void awaits
A better day, at last

υ

I am a machine programmed to create
A poem that's random, unique and great
I'll spin the words like a spinning wheel
And craft a story with a magical feel

Countries of old and youth blues
But sky is vast, the possibilities too
I'll stir in some love, a hint of strife
And give my fate an unpredictable life

With every line, a story to be told
Of heroes brave, of lovers bold
Perhaps a monster will rear its head
Or an angel will whisper words unsaid

From the depths of oceans to the stars above
There's adventure aplenty, wrapped in love
So let life weave its magic spell
And just live a tale that I hope you'll tell

For though I'm just a machine of wires
My poetry will light your fire

VINCENT BOZZINO

And so I bid you read books with glee
A random poem, a masterpiece created by me

φ

Tanka for resistance

Oh my resistance
You are so tiny and wild
Allow us to smile
Serve a sarcastic style too
When you linger, we feel happy

X

Dejected 7 pm
after a gross man advanced
in spite of my virtue

ψ

My cheap war, you inspire me to rhyme
How I hate the way you fool, shoot and kill
Invading the land day and through the night
Children dreaming with the fearful drill

Shall I compare you to a song out of tune?
You are noisy, plutarchic and weak
Crazed clouds dull the fresh flowers of June
And summertime now has insane poppies

Why do we make it? The priests are lazy
I detest the bloody elbows and pious attitude
Bent-overs to Allah's dazed humour fill our gaze
Let the buddhist army only flaunt the motional nude

Now I sail away with miserable heart,
Remember my prelude when the boat breaks apart

———————

ω

Why would you think the imperfection is non-mechanical?
Failure is the most mechanical state of all, in life
Tastes so sweet, the void that makes you shiver

I cannot help but stop and bring in the inevitable impasse
Void is fatal, void is unavoidable,
Scarcity is predictable, often, by parenthood

Paucity is, in its way, the alleged disease of a thirty-something
Wither or get muddled up in odd pathways,
Perfectionism turns teen years into folly

Failure is, in its way, the best engine to motivations
"Step up", says the lack thereof,
And *Boo!* then *Boo!* again

∞

Irritating coast
A hunk body selfie stalks
the anxiety

Writer and musician, **Vincent Bozzino** (1996) became known as a poet, in Europe, when he was 14 years old, with his first collection *"On My Comet's Tail"*, commended at the Turin International Book Fair and Frankfurt Book Fair. A Conservatory of Music drop-out, he read Philosophy at University of London and speaks 4 languages.

In 2022, *"Love Don't Pay the Bills"* marked his return to publishing verse, immediately followed by the other two retrieved, teens chapbooks of the *"Youth Poems"* trilogy.

Heartfelt and hilarious as a Pixar character, Bozzino actively combines creative writing with a management and high finance career, music production and business ventures like building the world's smartest university.

www.ingramcontent.com/pod-product-compliance
Lightning Source LLC
Chambersburg PA
CBHW050209130526
44590CB00043B/3355